Little Guy

Journey of hope

Emma Major

Little Guy

Journey of hope

Emma Major

wild goose
publications  www.ionabooks.com

Copyright © 2020 Emma Major

First published 2020 by
Wild Goose Publications,
21 Carlton Court, Glasgow G5 9JP, UK,
the publishing division of the Iona Community.
Scottish Charity No. SC003794. Limited Company Reg. No. SC096243.

ISBN 978-1-84952-740-8

All rights reserved. Apart from the circumstances described below relating to non-commercial use, no part of this publication may be reproduced in any form or by any means, including photocopying or any information storage or retrieval system, without written permission from the publisher.

Non-commercial use:
The material in this book may be used non-commercially for group work without written permission from the publisher.
Please make full acknowledgement of the source, together with mention of our website: www.ionabooks.com

Commercial or online use:
For any commercial or online use of the contents of this book, permission must be obtained in writing from Wild Goose Publications via PLSclear.com

Emma Major has asserted her right in accordance with the Copyright, Designs and Patents Act, 1988, to be identified as the author of this work.

Overseas distribution:
Australia: Willow Connection Pty Ltd, Unit 4A, 3-9 Kenneth Road, Manly Vale, NSW 2093
New Zealand: Pleroma, Higginson Street, Otane 4170, Central Hawkes Bay

Printed by Bell & Bain, Thornliebank, Glasgow

Introduction

I started writing poetry in childhood as a way of processing my emotions. I write poems most days, often many in a day. I have poems in a number of poetry collections and have produced several books of them.

I am a poet.

I am not an artist.

I have never been able to draw – my art teachers will confirm this. I lost most of my eyesight several years ago, making it even less likely that I would acquire that skill. Yet I woke up one day with the first three of these pictures and their poems in my mind; I knew that I had to get them onto paper.

In less than two weeks, 25 poems and drawings of 'Little Guy' had emerged.

I had an inkling this was God at work. Where else would this ability to draw suddenly have come from? However the sense of urgency didn't make a lot of sense.

Then, less than a month later, coronavirus appeared in the UK. We had to distance from each other; isolate, alone at home in a situation none of us have ever had to deal with.

Now the rush to get Little Guy onto paper makes sense.

Little Guy starts off anxious and depressed, before moving through hope and trust to a point where he is able to relate to the world and thrive again.

Little Guy journeys with us.

Pondering meaning
Life, universe, everything
Heavy feeling

Amidst millions
Loneliness epidemic
Restore connections

Could I fly away?
My wingspan insufficient
Feathers of my mind

Angels bring me back
From those claws of death
Moonlight shows the key

Floating peacefully
Leaving stress and strain behind
Catching calmness

Forest adventures
Lost as night falls – losing fear
Moonlit mystery

Swinging thoughtfully
Breathing deeply; thinking likewise
Looking for uplift

Taking time away
Shining a light on life's paths
Guided every step

Caught in a rainstorm
Could extinguish hope and joy
Umbrella protects

Noticing small joys
Umbrella from life's rainstorms
Hope in each moment

Achieving *shanti*
Peaceful, calm, serenity
Balloons aplenty

Thinking deeply
Underneath my shady tree
Resting gratefully

Singing joyfully
Not a care in the world
A lesson for me

Beyond those trees
World of opportunities
Just waiting for me

First time exploring
Anxiety-inducing
Nature is soothing

Waves gently lapping
Warm breezes cooling heat haze
Perfect peacefulness

Out of comfort zone
What an opportunity
Feelings of freedom

Lifting head and heart
Anxiety, fear, stress
Left them far below

Spiky on my own
Anxiety metaphor
I'm flowering now

Appear aloof
They rely on each other
A giraffe lesson

Reality hits
Home alone; but wait, a cat
Wonder whose he is

Slowly slowly
Works for cat's anxiety
Now he's trusting me

Peaceful company
Overcame anxiety
Swinging happily

Home alone no more
Life improved with company
World much less scary

Feeling brave today
Sat next to a stranger
Even had a chat

We both live alone
Might meet same time next week
Helping each other

Suggested a walk
Forest exploration
Walking and talking

Friends together
Holiday happiness
No longer alone

Sharing memories
The good and the bad times
True recovery

Bridge revisited
Facing bad memories
Hope recovered

About the author:

Emma Major is a mum, wife, friend, pioneer lay minister, blind wheelchair user and poet. She lives just outside Reading, UK, with dreams which roam much further afield, and a particular passion for Africa.

Emma has written poetry since childhood, most of it lost as notebooks have been thrown away. Since 2003 she has been sharing her poetry online on various social media platforms, most recently Instagram and Facebook. She has also posted other resources and reflections on ministry in her blog, LLM Calling (http://llmcalling.blogspot.com/).

Emma's poems have been included in several poetry collections; she has also produced two books of poetry, one about miscarriage and grief (*This Is My Story; This Is My Song*), the other about mental health (*An Alphabet of Mental Health*).

For each picture in the *Little Guy* book there is an audio description recorded by Emma to ensure that everyone can access it. These can be heard at:

https://www.youtube.com/playlist?list=PL8KIeTiwGOpUZzPXDOBX37KZVK7Kjjkwo

Wild Goose Publications, the publishing house of the Iona Community established in the Celtic Christian tradition of Saint Columba, produces books, e-books, CDs and digital downloads on:

- holistic spirituality
- social justice
- political and peace issues
- healing
- innovative approaches to worship
- song in worship, including the work of the Wild Goose Resource Group
- material for meditation and reflection

For more information:

Wild Goose Publications
The Iona Community
21 Carlton Court, Glasgow, G5 9JP, UK

Tel. +44 (0)141 429 7281
e-mail: admin@ionabooks.com

or visit our website at
www.ionabooks.com
for details of all our products and online sales